HOW·TO·DRAW

United States
HOT ROD
Association

MONSTER JAM ®

FEATURING

WORLD CHAMPIONSHIP WRESTLING ™

MONSTER TRUCKS

GRAVE DIGGER

by Michael Teitelbaum • illustrated by Ron Zalme

Troll

Special thanks to Liza Greenwald Abrams, Wally Cabreras, and Evelyn Caceres

A Creative Media Applications Production

Art Direction by Fabia Wargin Design

Troll

Published by Troll Communications L.L.C.

INTRODUCTION

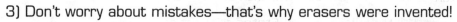

You've seen them climb over other trucks, crush cars, soar through the air in 100-foot leaps, and roar around the track. They're the coolest vehicles ever—the monster trucks. And now you get to draw these awesome machines with the wicked paint jobs!

Whether it's the flame-shooting American Guardian, the tiger-shaped Prowler, or the outrageous WCW trucks like Goldberg and Nitro Machine, you'll be bringing all the fuel-injected excitement of monster trucks to life by simply following the step-by-step instructions in this book.

Just as no one becomes a champion monster truck driver overnight, it also takes patience and practice to learn to draw. In both cases, you'll make some mistakes and experience some setbacks. But in the end, if you persevere and learn from your mistakes, you'll reach your goal—which in the case of this book is learning to draw your favorite monster trucks.

Here are a few things you should know before getting started:

1) Draw lightly as you sketch. You'll have plenty of time to darken your lines as you finish your drawing and fill in the details.

2) Stay loose! Let your hand and arm move freely. Don't grip your pencil like it's the steering wheel of King Krunch! Drawing should be fun and relaxing.

3) Don't worry about mistakes—that's why erasers were invented!

4) Practice, and be patient. It takes time to get good at drawing.

As you draw the trucks in this book, you'll see that all of them are made up of a few basic shapes, with some details added. If you can draw a circle, square, triangle, rectangle, and oval, you can draw a monster truck—lots of them, in fact!

MATERIALS

- medium pencil
- eraser
- 8 1/2" x 11" (21.5 x 28 cm) sheets of white paper

sphere

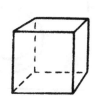
cube

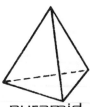
pyramid

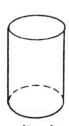
cylinder

cone

Let's begin.
Drivers, start your engines!
Artists, start your pencils!

3

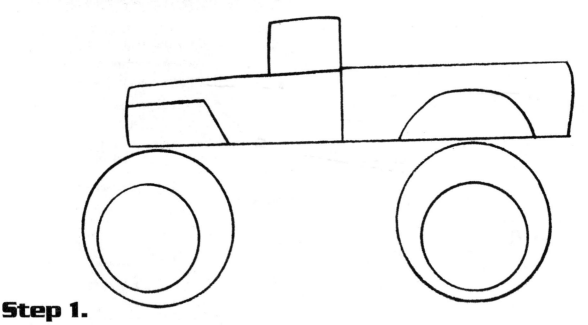

Step 1.

Begin with two long rectangles side by side. Notice that they're slightly curved on the ends. Draw a square for the cab on top of the left rectangle. Add the two lines shown on the left and a semicircle on the right for the wheel wells. The tires are two pairs of circles, one circle within the other.

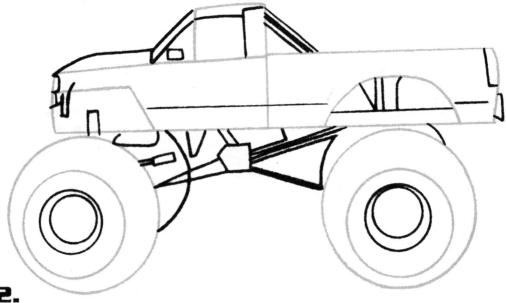

Step 2.

It's time to add some details. Draw in the windshield and roll bars. Add more details to the body and wheel wells, as shown. Then draw the chassis (the stuff under the body of the truck). Three curved lines form the right-hand wheels. Add four additional circles in the left-hand wheels to give them depth.

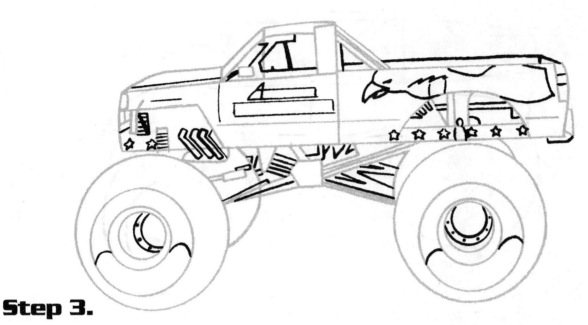

Step 3.

Now do the paint job—draw American Guardian's famous eagle, and outline the logo, as shown. Fill in additional details all over the truck. These are the toughest things to draw, so remember to work slowly and carefully.

Step 4.

Complete the letters of the logo, and add stars and stripes to the eagle. Give the tires a light tread. Compare your drawing with the finished picture of American Guardian, and fill in any remaining details. Blacken the areas shown. Darken the lines you want to keep, and erase the lines you don't need. American Guardian is ready to shoot out flames 25 feet long! (You can draw those in if you like!)

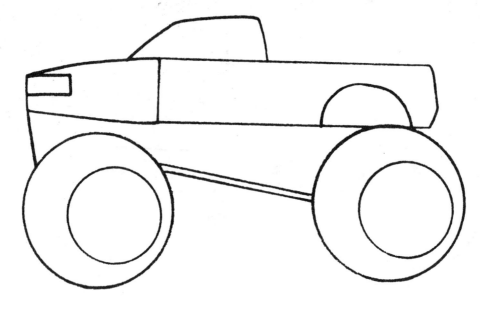

Step 1.

Start with a long rectangle for the body. Notice the curved back end. Add a narrow-nosed rectangular shape to the left of it to form the front of the truck. Copy the shape on top to create the cab, then place a small rectangle at the very front of the body for the headlight. Draw a semicircle toward the back for the wheel well. Then draw two large circles, each with a smaller circle inside, to form the wheels. Add a straight line from the front of the body to the front wheel. Finish this step with two parallel lines connecting the wheels. These will form the bottom of the chassis.

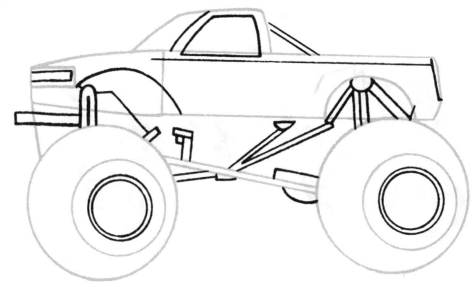

Step 2.

Time for the details. Draw the windshield and roll bar. Add more details to the body, as shown, then draw the chassis. Complete this step by drawing four additional circles to give the wheels some depth.

Step 3.

In step 3, continue to add details to the cab and body, including an outline of the logo. Complete the chassis and the left wheels, and draw the right ones, as shown.

Step 4.

Let's paint this baby! Add the Destroyer logo and the flames on the front of the truck. Give the tires some tread. Compare your drawing with the finished picture of Destroyer, and fill in any remaining details. Blacken the areas shown. Darken the lines you want to keep, and erase the lines you don't need. Destroyer is ready to take a wheelie walk across the tops of crushed cars!

SURVIVOR™

Step 1.

Start with a long rectangle. Now add a square to the right of that and a sloping rectangular shape to the right of that. These three shapes form the body. Copy the two shapes above to create the cab. Add two curved lines on the body to form the wheel wells. Draw two large circles with a smaller circle inside each one to form the tires. Two parallel lines between the tires will help you position the chassis.

Step 2.

Detail time. Draw the windshield and window, and then the narrow rectangles that form the grill. Add more details to the body, as shown, and draw the chassis. Add more circles within the right tires to give them dimension, and draw the two left tires.

Step 3.

Continue adding details to the cab and body, and sketch out the shape of the logo. Complete the chassis, and add a few more details to the wheels.

Step 4.

Outline the letters of the Survivor logo, and draw a thick tread on the tires. Compare your drawing with the finished picture of Survivor, and add any remaining details. Blacken the areas shown. Darken the lines you want to keep, and erase the lines you don't need. Survivor is ready to tear it up at a monster truck event!

Step 1.

Begin with a large rectangular shape for the body, slanting slightly downward. Add a smaller rectangular shape to the left for the hood. Draw two curved lines for the wheel wells. The tires come next—two pairs of circles, one circle within the other. Notice that the tires overlap the wheel wells slightly.

Step 2.

Let's place the details. Add the windshield, windows, and headlights. Start to draw the chassis—which is visible under the truck, as well as through the high wheel wells. Sketch in the logo and the first few flames of WCW Nitro Machine's fiery 3-D paint job. Add three lines across the body between the wheel wells, and an additional circle on

each wheel.

Step 3.

Continue to add details to the cab and body, including some more flames. Then complete the chassis and the wheels (don't forget the cool hubcaps).

Step 4.

Fill in the logo, and draw lots more flames all over the body. Give the tires some tread. Compare your drawing with the finished picture of WCW Nitro Machine, and add any remaining details. Blacken the areas shown. Darken the lines you want to keep, and erase the lines you don't need. WCW Nitro Machine is ready to roar into slammin', jammin' action!

11

Step 1.

Start off with a small rectangle (note the slight curve on the left edge). Add two slanted rectangular shapes to the right to form the body. Connect the left and right rectangles with a slanted straight line. Draw the small triangular shape to the right of the body to form the fender. Two curves for the wheel wells come next. Draw a guideline below the body to help you place the tires, and connect this guideline to the body with two straight vertical lines. Next, draw the tire shapes, as shown—three large ovals with three smaller ovals inside.

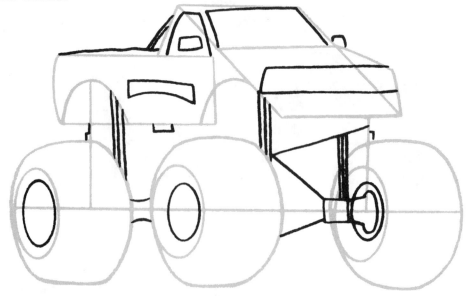

Step 2.

Time for details. Complete the truckbed, then add the windshield, window, side mirrors, and grill. Begin the logo on the door. Finish step 2 by drawing the chassis and adding two more ovals to the wheels.

Step 3.

Continue adding details to the cab, body, chassis, and tires. Don't forget the mountain range logo.

Step 4.

Outline the letters of the logo on the door, and give the tires some tread. Compare your drawing with the finished picture of Mountaineer, and fill in any remaining details. Blacken the areas shown. Darken the lines you want to keep, and erase the lines you don't need. Mountaineer is ready for car-crushing madness!

PREDATOR®

Step 1.

Begin with the body, which is roughly rectangular in shape. But notice how it curves in slightly on the left and slants down on the right to form the panther-shaped front hood. Add the cab shape, as shown, on top of the body shape, and then draw two curved lines for the wheel wells. Three circles form the wheels, and each one gets an oval shape inside for the rims. Notice that the rear wheel touches the body. Connect the right-hand tires with two parallel lines to form the bottom of the chassis.

Step 2.

Now let's take care of some details. Draw in the windshield and the chassis. Add two more ovals to the right-hand wheels, and draw a curved line for the left rear tire. Complete this step by sketching in the panther face on the front of Predator—don't forget the fangs!

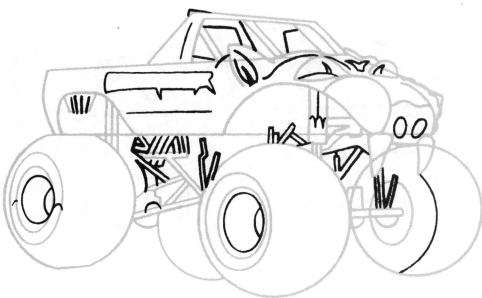

Step 3.

Continue to fill in cab and body details. Complete the eyes, ear, and nostrils of the panther, then sketch in an outline to help position the logo. Finish off the chassis and the wheels, as shown.

Step 4.

Fill in the letters of the logo, and add some stripes to the panther face. Give the tires a good tread. Compare your drawing with the finished picture of Predator, and add any remaining details. Blacken the areas shown. Darken the lines you want to keep, and erase the lines you don't need. This big cat is ready to pounce!

PROWLER™

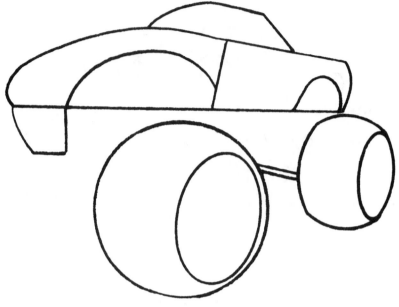

Step 1.

Begin with a rectangular shape that has a curved right edge for the body. Add the sweeping front end, as shown. Place the cab shape on top, then draw two curved lines for the wheel wells and the fang shape below the body on the left. Add the wheel and rim shapes—two large ovals with two smaller ovals inside—and place two parallel lines between the tires.

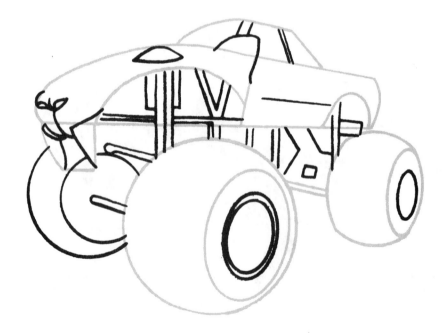

Step 2.

Start adding details to the cab and body, including Prowler's tigerlike eye, nose, and fangs. Draw the chassis, as shown, and the right front wheel. Add two more ovals to the left front wheel, and one to the rear.

16

Step 3.

Continue to add details to the cab and body—don't forget the tiger's ear! Outline the logo on the door. Complete the chassis, and add a few more details to the wheels.

Step 4.

In the final step, complete the logo, give the tires some tread, and draw lots of tiger stripes. Compare your drawing with the finished picture of Prowler, and fill in any remaining details. Blacken the areas shown. Darken the lines you want to keep, and erase the lines you don't need. Prowler is ready to hunt—monster trucks, that is!

MADUSA™

Step 1.

Begin with a rectangle, slanting upward, then add two more rectangular shapes to the right to complete the body. Notice how these shapes curve down to form the front end. Place the cab shape above the body, and draw a curved line for the rear wheel well. Add two pairs of circles for the wheel and rim shapes, overlapping the truck body slightly in the rear. Draw two parallel lines and then a third line between the wheels to help you place the chassis.

Step 2.

Time for some details. Draw the window and windshield, the front wheel well, and the front and rear bumpers. Complete the chassis and the two left tires, and add two more circles to the right tires.

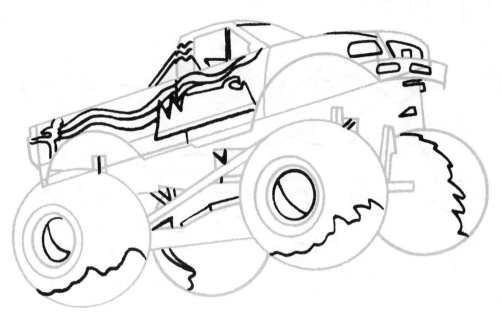

Step 3.

Continue adding details to the cab and the front end. Next, let's work on the paint job—draw Madusa's wavy snake pattern along the side, and outline the logo on the door. Finally, complete the chassis and the wheels, as shown.

Step 4.

Finish filling in the logo, and give the tires some tread. Compare your drawing with the finished picture of Madusa, and add any remaining details. Blacken the areas shown. Darken the lines you want to keep, and erase the lines you don't need. Madusa is ready to take on all challengers!

19

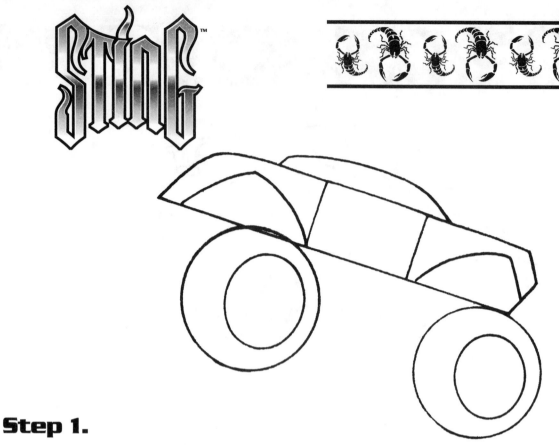

Step 1.

Start with a small rectangle, slanting downward. Add the rectangular shapes shown to the left and right to form the body. A long curved line above forms the cab. Add the wheel wells, as shown, then draw two large circles with smaller circles inside to form the wheels and rims.

Step 2.

Add details to the cab and body, and start to sketch in the chassis. Draw the two right-hand wheels, and add two more circles to the left.

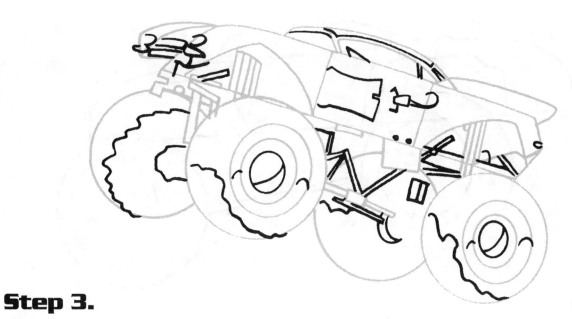

Step 3.

Continue to fill in details on the cab and body, and outline the logo on the door. Complete the chassis and the wheels, as shown.

Step 4.

Draw in the logo and scorpion graphic, and add a heavy tread to the tires. Compare your drawing with the finished picture of Sting, and fill in any remaining details. Blacken the areas shown. Darken the lines you want to keep, and erase the lines you don't need. Watch out for Sting's scorpion's tail! Don't get stung!

Step 1.

Begin with a rectangular shape, then draw the two additional body shapes on either side. Add the cab above, and two more rectangular shapes for the wheel wells. Two pairs of circles, one circle inside the other, make the tires and rims. Notice that the larger circles overlap the body. Finish this step by drawing two parallel lines between the wheels to place the chassis.

Step 2.

Add details to the cab and body, as shown. Start to draw the chassis, and the two right-hand wheels. Add two more circles to each of the left-hand wheels.

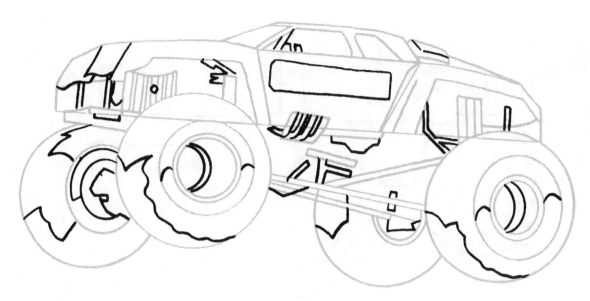

Step 3.

Start this step by adding details to the cab and front end. Then outline the logo on the door. Draw the side pipes, and complete the chassis and wheels.

Step 4.

Fill in the logo, and give the tires some tread. Compare your drawing with the finished picture of Goldberg, and add any remaining details. Blacken the areas shown. Darken the lines you want to keep, and erase the lines you don't need. Goldberg is ready to be challenged! Who's next?

AVENGER™

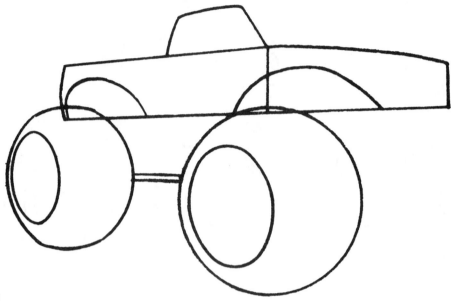

Step 1.

Start with two rectangular shapes for the body. Notice that the one on the right curves down across the top. Add another rectangular shape for the cab and two curved lines for the wheel wells. Two ovals, slightly overlapping the body, form the wheels. Place a smaller oval inside each wheel for the rims. Two parallel lines connect the wheels and form the bottom of the chassis.

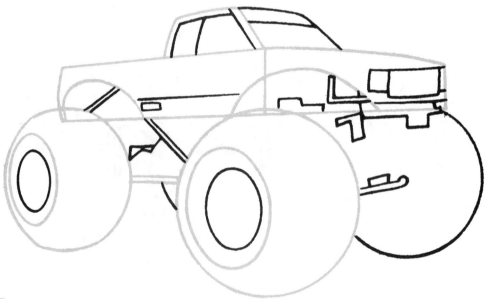

Step 2.

Add the window and windshield shapes next. Then fill in details on the body and start to draw the chassis. Add an interior oval to the wheels you drew in step 1, and draw a half-circle for the left front tire.

24

Step 3.

Once you've added a few more details to the cab and body, it's time to start the paint job. Cover the body with flames, and sketch in an outline to help position the Avenger logo. Complete the chassis, and add the details shown to the wheels.

Step 4.

Finish off the logo, and give the tires some tread. Compare your drawing with the finished picture of Avenger, and fill in any remaining details. Blacken the areas shown. Darken the lines you want to keep, and erase the lines you don't need. Avenger is ready to torch all opponents!

KING KRUNCH™

Step 1.

Begin with a long rectangle, then add the three rectangular shapes on the right to form the body. Draw the cab shape next, followed by the wheel wells. Add two circles for the wheels, slightly overlapping the body, and an oval within each circle for the rims. Draw an "L" shape from the center of the body to the front wheel to help place the chassis.

Step 2.

In this step, add the windshield, windows, and grill. Begin to draw the chassis, then outline the two left-hand wheels. Add two more ovals to each wheel on the right.

Step 3.

Fill in the details on the cab and body. Sketch in an outline to help position the King Krunch logo. Complete the chassis and wheels, as shown.

Step 4.

Draw in the logo. Complete the grill, and add some tread to the tires. Compare your drawing with the finished picture of King Krunch, and fill in any remaining details. Blacken the areas shown. Darken the lines you want to keep, and erase the lines you don't need. King Krunch is ready to crunch down on a truck or two!

Step 1.

Start with a large rectangular shape, slanting upward, for the body. Add a smaller rectangular shape for the hood. Two curved lines form the wheel wells. Add the two shapes shown below the body to help place the chassis. Then draw two circles for the tires and two ovals inside the circles for the rims. Use two parallel lines to connect the rear wheel to the chassis.

Step 2.

Complete the roof, windshield, and hood. Add a small rectangle for the window. Continue drawing the chassis, then add a half-circle for the left front tire. Draw two more ovals on the right wheels.

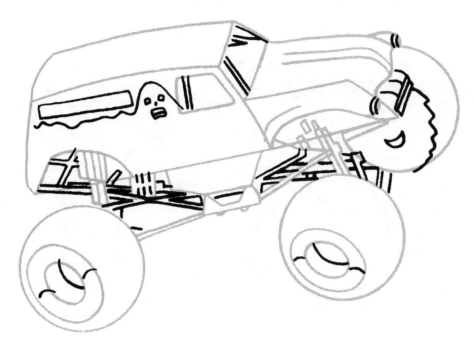

Step 3.

Continue adding details to the cab and body. Outline the logo, and begin to draw Grave Digger's ghostly paint job. Complete the chassis, and add a few more details to the wheels.

Step 4.

Finish off the ghostly paint job, and draw the Grave Digger logo. Add some tread to the tires. Compare your drawing with the finished picture of Grave Digger, and fill in any remaining details. Blacken the areas shown. Darken the lines you want to keep, and erase the lines you don't need. Grave Digger is ready to dig a grave for the other trucks in monster truck events!

WILD THANG™

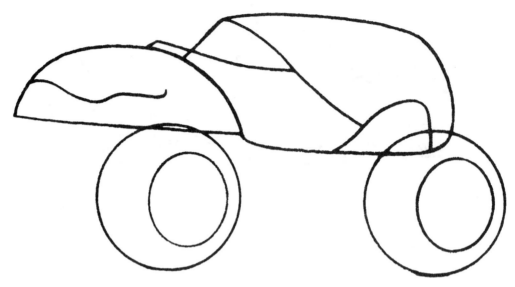

Step 1.

The shape of this skull on wheels is more rounded than any of the other trucks in this book. Begin with a half-circle for the front end, then copy the remaining shapes to form the body and windshield, as shown. These shapes are complicated, so work slowly and carefully. Add a wavy line across the half-circle. Next, draw two large circles for the tires, overlapping the body slightly. Add a smaller circle within each tire for the rims.

Step 2.

Detail time! Add lots of wavy lines to the body, as shown, to really bring out the skull shape. Then start to draw the chassis and the two right-hand tires. Add more circles to the left-hand tires to give them dimension.

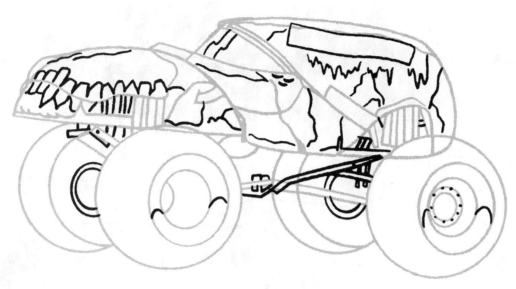

Step 3.

In this step, draw the teeth and other "cracked bone" details. Sketch in a outline to help position the logo. Complete the chassis, and add a few more details to the wheels.

Step 4.

Complete the logo, and finish decorating the skull. Add some tread to the tires. Compare your drawing with the finished picture of Wild Thang, and fill in any remaining details. Blacken the areas shown. Darken the lines you want to keep, and erase the lines you don't need. Wild Thang is ready to go flying over all competitors!

ANY LAST REQUESTS?

BRING IT ON!!!!